INTERLAKE
GUIDE

Discover the Ultimate Alpine Jewel of
Switzerland: Your Updated, Comprehensive
Manual to Top Attractions, Fun outdoor
activities, and Hidden Gems.

Rick Cage

Table of Content

Conclusion

Chapter 1

Introduction to Interlaken

Visitors are enthralled by the stunning landscape, colorful culture, and unrivaled outdoor experiences that can be found in Interlaken, a town that is tucked away in the center of Switzerland. Interlaken, which is located between Lake Thun and Lake Brienz, is a gateway to the magnificent Bernese Oberland area, which allows visitors to experience the ideal combination of natural beauty and Swiss allure.

The name "Interlaken" comes from the fact that the city is situated in a strategic "between the lakes." A picture-perfect location can be found in Interlaken, which is characterized by the azure waters of Lake Thun to the west and the sparkling expanse of Lake

Brienz to the east. The town itself is distinguished by its picturesque lanes that are lined with classic Swiss chalets, colorful flower boxes, and breathtaking views of the Alps that are located in the immediate surrounding area.

Brief History of Interlaken

There are artifacts from the Neolithic periods that have been unearthed here in recent years, along with some coins from the days of the Romans. The earliest settlements were established in the area surrounding Interlaken as far back as the late Stone Age and the Bronze Age. More recently, in the early part of the 12th century, a new community was founded, but it was not until 1275 that historical papers of history began to reference this region, notably the adjacent mountain hamlet of Habkern.

Interlaken was termed 'Aarmuhle' for many centuries, after the riverbank mill, and this name remained right up to the year 1891. During the 1130s, an abbey for the Augustinian Canons was constructed, which led to the development of the town in the vicinity of the Aare River.

THE ABBEY FOR THE INTERLAKEN

The early abbey had an essential part in the foundation of the town and it was very much preserved by Lothair III, a Holy Roman Emperor. It became vital to the local population and some women were residing here by the middle of the 13th century.

Interlaken Abbey increased in prestige and eventually governed over more than 20 nearby churches, and by the 14th century, around 400 people were living here, made up of some 50 monks and priests, with the remainder being women and nuns. Weekly markets were soon the rule of the day, enabling villagers to exchange and barter their products, which included butter, cheese, and sheep.

The stringent monastic norms were notably weakened during the later half of the 14th century and the clergy started to see considerable infighting and different arguments, which were frequently violent. Some convents were dissolved in the 15th century and during the Protestant Reformation of the 1520s, unrest occurred. The days of the abbey were numbered when the Interlaken bailiwick was created, with the monastery being utilized for administrative reasons, as well as a temporary hospital, a granary, and even as a location to store wine.

QUARRELS DURING THE 16TH, 17TH, AND 18TH CENTURIES

Interlaken (then Aarmuhle) started to contest possession of the surrounding forests and fields, with adjacent Matten claiming rights to this territory as well. This constant quarreling persisted for over three centuries, despite countless futile efforts at mediation. In 1810, the two towns ultimately agreed to share the land evenly and this long-running struggle ended, marking the start of a more fruitful and tranquil era of history for Interlaken.

A SURPRISING TIME FOR TOURISM

In the early 19th century, a new commerce in tourism was starting to make itself known, due in no little part to the superb paintings of regional landscapes being created at the time by famous Swiss painters, such as Franz Niklaus Konig (1765 to 1832).

First held in 1805, the Unspunnenfest celebration highlighted Swiss culture and also served to place Interlaken on the tourist map. Visitors traveled from all across Europe in search of mountain air, luxury hotels, and spas. Built-in 1864, the Victoria Jungfrau Grand Hotel provides the complete package -

elegance, unobstructed mountain views, beautiful gardens, and contemporary conveniences.

The Interlaken to Darligen railway line was established in 1872 and was subsequently expanded, ensuring that the town had never been simpler to visit. Hotels immediately sprouted up all around the town, with the most attractive providing views of the Bernese Alps and the Jungfrau peak in particular. A factory for the weaving of wool was built in the 1920s, after the conclusion of the First World War. However, following the Second World War, it was not until the 1950s that the tourist sector began to steadily revive, when the town started to be utilized as a base for significant international conferences.

THE TOWN TODAY

Tourism in Interlaken is as robust as it has ever been. A trip down the town's main artery, the Hoheweg, will uncover numerous tempting gift stores and attractions. A tranquil walk along the shores of Lake Thun is advised, or maybe a climb to the peak of the Harder Klum Mountain aboard the funicular train termed the Harderbahn.

For history aficionados seeking Swiss heritage, the Tourist Museum of the Jungfrau Region (Touristik Museum der Jungfrau region) on the Obere Gasse may be of interest. Others merely come here for cross-country skiing and snowboarding in the winter months.

Why Visit Interlaken?

Interlaken's attractiveness rests in its unsurpassed natural beauty and availability of outdoor activities. Whether you're a thrill-seeker desiring adrenaline-pumping thrills or a nature lover seeking calm among gorgeous surroundings, Interlaken has something for everyone.

For adrenaline addicts, Interlaken is a wonderland of adventure sports. From skydiving over the snow-capped peaks of the Jungfrau area to paragliding high above the emerald-green valleys, the town offers an assortment of heart-pounding sports sure to get your adrenaline racing. For those wanting a more leisurely pace, Interlaken's gorgeous lakes and thick woods offer the ideal setting for hiking, bicycling, and picnics.

Moreover, Interlaken provides a perfect base for exploring the surrounding area. With easy access to classic places such as the Jungfrau, Schilthorn, and Grindelwald, guests may go on thrilling day excursions to view some of Switzerland's most stunning landscapes.

Beyond its natural beauty, Interlaken enjoys a rich cultural past. The town is home to several museums, galleries, and cultural events that reflect Switzerland's distinctive history and culture. From traditional Swiss folklore performances to modern art exhibits, there's always something going on in Interlaken to engage your mind.

In addition to its outdoor experiences and cultural attractions, Interlaken provides a warm and inviting ambiance that keeps people coming back year after year. Whether you're eating a wonderful Swiss fondue at a quaint alpine restaurant or walking down the promenade admiring the views, you'll discover that Interlaken's charm is as tempting as its surroundings.

In short, Interlaken is a place like no other, where natural beauty, adventure, and culture merge to produce a unique experience. Whether you're seeking thrills, leisure, or cultural immersion, Interlaken offers it all, making it the ideal place for your next Swiss vacation.

Chapter 2

Planning Your Trip to Interlaken

Best Time to Visit

- **Peak Season**: Summer (June to August) is the busiest season in Interlaken. Just like other Swiss towns, Interlaken heats up dramatically throughout summer. The enticing warmth attracts people outside as the trails come alive with activity. Both the lakefronts buzz with people partaking in different activities while the city's streets are packed with visitors. This is also the rainiest season of the bunch, although it rains at sporadic intervals, not enough to interrupt your plans. Hotel reservations are tough to come by in this busy season, so book yours early or you may not be able to locate one.

- **Shoulder Season**: The in-between seasons of Spring (March to May) and Autumn (September to November) are quite vacant in Interlaken. If there's any convention or conference planned during these seasons, you could encounter the participants around town. Otherwise, there's no rush at tourist places and you may explore the city in relative tranquility. Late spring and early fall are still suitable for outdoor activities including hiking, cycling excursions, canyoning, and kayaking. But paragliding and bathing in the lakes will most definitely remain restricted till summer. Enquire ahead about reservations or you may lose your accommodation to a conference attendee.

- **Low Season**: Winter (December to February) is undoubtedly a low season in Interlaken. And by low we mean there will scarcely be any visitors around. But their position will be replaced by adrenaline addicts and thrill seekers who throng to the powdered slopes for the thrilling rush of skiing and snowboarding. If you decide to visit Interlaken during this season, you will get fantastic bargains on your accommodation and virtually no crowds at tourist locations. On the flip side, most of the outdoor activities will be closed for the season and will leave you with a reduced agenda.

Interlaken In Spring (March To May):

Temperature - Spring rarely seems like spring in Interlaken with temperatures ranging from -3 to 10°C. But it progressively begins warming up towards the end.

- **Weather** - The first two months of spring seem a little different from winter. The subzero temps may restrict you inside and play spoilsport with your plans. Snow is replaced by rain, which adds to the weather's cool impact.

- **Significance** - Interlaken begins taking on a green cover even as the neighboring mountains remain blanketed in snow. The city starts opening up gradually to welcome the summer that follows. You will discover more and more attractions and tourist locations opening their doors for business. But the trekking paths remain blocked until all the snow is gone. You may climb onto a cable car or a funicular and make your way to the summit for some wonderful vistas.

- **Why you should visit today** - Interlaken is frigid in this season and many companies do not open until the end. Your days will primarily be spent inside, either in one of the numerous museums or simply relaxing around your hotel room. But if this is your idea of a great holiday, then Interlaken will welcome you with open arms. Although, if you've ever wanted to try skiing or ice skating, now would be the ideal time to do it. The Ballenberg Open-Air Diving Museum is highly recommended for its accurate representation of rural Swiss life. Old structures from all across the county were moved and restored here as a part of a permanent display. Actors in period-appropriate clothes give further flair to the proceedings. A lake cruise is another fantastic way to spend a cool spring day. Though it may become chilly at the lake, the breathtaking vistas of the surrounding mountains more than makeup for the effort. Towards the end of the season, when you may wander outside safely, visit the waterfalls near Interlaken. Visit the Reichenbach Falls, which were immortalized in a Sherlock Holmes novel. You have a 30-minute trek following a funicular trip to the base camp. Rent a Trötti scooter on your way down for a thrilling experience.

- **Things to know before the visit** - Spring will still be chilly and you will need to take a heavy jacket to guard against the cold. Be ready for an immediate change of plans if the weather plays truant. Keep an open agenda, and with an open mind, and you will truly appreciate Interlaken in spring.

- **Tips** - Along with a heavy jacket, be sure you take snow-proof shoes. These will come in handy if you face thick snow on mountain peaks. Dress in layers so that you can readily react to changing weather.

Interlaken In Summer (June To August)

- **Temperature** - Summer sees a waweatherake over the town, which is a comfort after a frigid spring. The temperature remains from 10 to 18°C.

- **Weather** - The bright days drive away the last of the spring chill. The mild weather clears even the high passes allowing them free for exploration. But this is also the city's wettest season, so you can anticipate inopportune periods of rain while you're out and about.

- **Significance** - Summer sees Interlaken in full bloom and all that the city has to offer is accessible without exception. As the pathways open up and wildflowers dot the slopes, your treks are accompanied by some of the most breathtaking vistas you will ever set your eyes on.

- **Why you should come now** - Interlaken provides you with more possibilities throughout the summer. You are free to attempt any activity without being constrained by the weather. The lakefronts are humming with activity as swimming and wakeboarding appear to be the major activities surrounding the lake. You may also utilize a restored steam paddle boat for touring the lake and revealing undiscovered beaches. You'll now be able to enjoy biking and paragliding as part of your outdoor pursuits. You can experience some of the greatest paragliding in Interlaken in July.

You may visit the museums for some quality inside time. Interlaken boasts quite a variety of museums that showcase various parts of the city's history and heritage. The 'World of the Great Aletsch Glacier' is an interactive exhibit that uncovers the mysteries of Europe's largest glacier which is 23 km long. The 'Jungfrau Park - The Fascinating Mysteries of the World' enables you to be a part of the displays for new insights. It does a terrific job of sparking your interest and giving a more immersive experience.

Summer also comes with an array of events that lend color and happiness to the summer air. One such event is the William Tell festival when amateurs dress up in medieval clothes and perform Schiller's renowned play.

With so many possibilities, it is little surprise therefore that summer is the busiest season in Interlaken.

- **Things to know before the visit** - The hotel charges go up in summer and the cost of traveling also grows dearer. But even finding lodging may prove to be a struggle. So, book your hotels in advance and you may also receive savings on your reservations. Also, make sure you confirm your reservations before you get up at the hotel.

- **Tips** - Light summer attire and a pair of sturdy hiking boots can come in helpful as you tackle the paths around the countryside. Always bring a water bottle with you and do not forget to carry a cap or a hat to protect your head from the sun.

Interlaken In fall (September To November):

- **Temperature** - As fall comes in after summer, it banishes the warmth and starts to prepare Interlaken for its bitter winter. The temperatures average from 0 and 14°C.

- **Weather** - The mercury starts falling at a steady rate and the rain adds its chill to the air. Though it doesn't rain as fiercely as in summer, it is enough to cool down the air. While early fall is not too awful, the later half becomes pretty chilly.

- **Significance** - The summer visitors wave farewell to Interlaken along with the season. As the city empties, it starts settling down for the winter. Many hotels and businesses shut down early owing to the weather and the lack of visitors. But, on the positive side, you virtually have the city to yourself.

- **Why you should visit today** - Interlaken is a different beast in October. After all the noise and activity of the high season, the city has a peaceful aura that makes it feel like a different city entirely. This is the best time to discover the city's culture and history in its various museums. Autumn is also the season of grape harvest and you may engage in some epicurean hobbies driven by the harvest season. The town of Spiez plays home to the annual grape harvest procession. Children dance in the streets dressed as grapes.

A decorated vehicle, escorted by a brass band, carried casks of wine. It is quite a show that needs to be witnessed first-hand. As the days become shorter, the higher passes and trails begin to close down around October. The hillsides are alight with diverse shades of reds, golds, oranges, and yellows before the trees shed their leaf for winter.

You may see a 300-year-old gastronomic tradition of celebratory cow drive, in September. Herds of cattle being led down from the highlands for 'apportioning of the cheese'. Locals dress up in traditional Swiss costumes to honor the occasion. But the nicest part of this ritual is the authentic Swiss cheese that you get to sample at the conclusion.

- **Things to know before the visit** - As the city empties out you will observe the accommodation costs decline and travel become pocket-friendlier. The hiking routes will stay open until October, following which they will be shut down for winter.

- **Tips** - The temperature changes substantially across the season. So, depending on what time you're traveling, pack a suitable jacket and dress in layers. A pair of durable boots will always come in useful.

Interlaken In Winter (December To February):

- **Temperature** - Interlaken enjoys classic Alpine weather with subzero temperatures and tons of snow. The temperatures normally range between -5 to 1°C.
- **Weather** - The weather stays cool throughout the season, although January and February experience the lowest temperatures. It becomes considerably colder in the mountains thanks to the frigid winds high above.
- **Significance** - Skiing, snowboarding, and ice skating are the attractions of winter in Interlaken. As the city hides behind a veil of snow, it is time to go home and savor the boiling-hot gastronomic pleasures on offer.

- **Why you should visit today** - This is a bit of a conflicting season in Interlaken. While the winter cold assures that no visitors remain behind, it nevertheless becomes busy with the professional daredevils who heed the call of the slopes. In the hotels and resorts near the slopes, the costs will climb and their availability will go down substantially. But in the city, the prices will be more cheap since it will be a bit desolate. One significant outdoor event that occurs in winter is the Christmas market. These customary get-togethers provide residents with an opportunity to catch up with friends. Young and old delight themselves with holiday delicacies such as cakes, eggnog, and biscuits. If you're seeking excitement, hit the slopes and take a lesson or two. It's quite simple if you get the hang of it. Otherwise, simply organize your days around museums. If weather allows you may even take a cable car to mountain summits and indulge yourself in the wonderful sights. Surprisingly several paragliding series remain active even in winter. Enjoy the excitement of soaring across a snow-covered landscape appearing like another universe.

- **Things to know before the visit** - Some parts of Interlaken will be busy and the hotel fees will be expensive. With a little search online you may snag a nice discount on your travel and hotel.

- **Tips** - Carry your thickest woolens and adequately robust shoes. A thermal suit will help you remain warmer. Remember, if you have snow in your boots, remove your wet socks immediately. A nice pair of sunglasses will shield your eyes from the ice glare and a good moisturizer will protect your skin. Interlaken is a town with a truly Swiss heart. With a vast and colorful past, it has many tales to tell. If you've picked your time of travel, book your Interlaken trip online. For a more customized trip, come into your closest Thomas Cook branch.

How to Get to Interlaken

How To Reach By Air

Interlaken doesn't have an airport. The closest airport is the International Airport in Bern. Getting to Interlaken from Bern takes 45 minutes by car and an hour and a half by rail. Alternatively, you may also go to Zurich Airport, and from there, you can catch a train from the airport straight to Interlaken. It takes roughly two hours to get from Zurich to Interlaken. Both Bern and Zurich are linked to international flights while Zurich is more popular for travelers arriving from outside Europe.

How To Reach By Bus

There are private buses from destinations like Munich, Paris, Florence, and Rome to Interlaken. The operators for these services are named Bus2alps. Some schedules indicate the frequency of the buses. However, February and March are busy seasons since more people are arriving for winter activities.

How To Reach By Car

For those who enjoy road vacations, the road travel from Zurich to Interlaken is fantastic. It is roughly 120 km and the roads are fantastic. However, if you are driving a rental vehicle, please be aware that the overnight parking prices in Interlaken are rather steep.

How To Reach By Rail

The best method to go to Interlaken would be via train. Interlaken has two stations - Interlaken OST (East) and West. The station is well-connected to the rest of Switzerland, from towns such as Zurich, Basel, Geneva, Bern, and Luzern. Interlaken West is closer to the city core however most trains will stop at both stops. Traveling to Interlaken by rail provides some magnificent panoramas and lovely views that are certainly pretty remarkable.

Transportation inside Interlaken

- **By Bus**:Many local buses may be utilized to convey people to different regions of the town. Typically, the hotel where you are staying will offer a visitor travel card which you may use to navigate about the city for free on buses and trains.
- **By Taxis**: There are various car-rental firms as well as taxi services which may be utilized to go about in Interlaken.

- **By Train**: Traveling anywhere locally in Switzerland is fairly simple owing to the incredibly efficient Swiss Metro. It's also extremely inexpensive and it's a wonderful benefit if you buy the Swiss pass since it will offer you some neat discounts.

- **By Bicycle:**Since Interlaken is a tiny town, it's simple to move about on bikes. There are rental businesses from whom you can acquire all types of bikes such as road bikes, all-terrain bikes, and e-bikes for hire.

- **By Foot**: The picturesque town of Interlaken is relatively tiny and it's pretty pleasant to go around and discover all the various sites here.

- **By Horse Carriage:** Quaint and quaint, you may also take a trip on a horse carriage and experience the old-world type of vibe as you move about the town at a slower speed.

Swiss Travel Pass

- Buy the Swiss Half Fare Card: Switzerland trains, buses, and cable cars are EXPENSIVE! I discovered the easiest method to travel inexpensively was to get the Swiss Half-Fare Card before I came. It provides you with 50% off every ordinary rail, bus, and even many cable cars. It only costs USD 150 but pays itself off in only a few days with several rail tickets in Switzerland costing close to $100 alone. If you are staying for more than 5 days, I advise getting the Swiss Half-Fare Card.

- Alternative 2: Buy the Swiss Travel Pass: The second alternative is to acquire the Swiss Travel Pass, which offers you unlimited rail, bus, and (many) cable car trips but it's rather pricey at roughly USD 100 each day so if you don't travel each day it isn't worth it.

- Alternative 3: Buy the FLEXI Swiss Travel Pass: The last (BEST) alternative is to obtain the FLEXI Swiss Travel Pass, which enables you to buy 8 days' worth of travel but you may pick the night before whether you want to activate the following day. That way you don't need to travel every day to receive your money's worth, you can simply activate the FLEXI Swiss Travel Pass on the days when you are undertaking significant transits. My advice is to book the Swiss Half-Fare Card or the FLEXI Swiss Travel Pass in advance before your vacation so it's ready to go when you arrive.

Packing Tips

When preparing for your vacation to Interlaken, it's crucial to consider the varied activities and weather conditions you may face. Here are some packing recommendations to help you prepare for your adventure:

1. **Layered Clothing**: Interlaken's weather may be unpredictable, so carrying layers is necessary. Bring lightweight clothes that can be readily layered for warmth, like long-sleeve shirts, sweaters, and a waterproof jacket.
2. **Comfortable Footwear**: Whether you're climbing in the mountains or touring the town on foot, comfortable and durable footwear is essential. Pack hiking boots or walking shoes with adequate grip to tackle difficult terrain.

3. **Rain Gear**: Don't forget to carry a waterproof jacket or poncho, as well as an umbrella, to remain dry during unexpected rains or when visiting waterfalls and lakeshores.

4. **Sun Protection:** Even on foggy days, the sun in the Swiss Alps may be intense. Be sure to take sunglasses, a wide-brimmed hat, and sunscreen with a high SPF to protect your skin from UV radiation.

5. **Backpack**: A lightweight and robust backpack is necessary for carrying basics such as water bottles, food, a camera, and a map when exploring the outdoors.

6. **Travel Adapter**: Switzerland utilizes Type C and Type J electrical outlets, so be sure to take a universal travel adapter to power your electronic gadgets.

7. **Camera Gear**: Interlaken's breathtaking vistas are a photographer's delight, so don't

forget to carry your camera, additional batteries, memory cards, and a tripod to capture the splendor of the Swiss Alps.

8. **Reusable Water Bottle**: Stay hydrated when touring Interlaken by carrying a reusable water bottle. Tap water in Switzerland is safe to drink, so you may refill your bottle at fountains and public taps around the town.

9. **Swiss Francs**: While credit cards are generally accepted in Interlaken, it's always a good idea to bring some Swiss Francs for little purchases, gratuities, and souvenirs.

10. **Travel Documents**:Finally, don't forget to bring your passport, travel insurance documentation, and any essential visas or permits for your trip to Interlaken. Keep these essentials in a waterproof and secure travel wallet or bag for convenient access.

Chapter 3

Where to Stay in Interlaken (Top Hotels)

The 4 Most Highly-Rated Luxury Hotels In Interlaken

VICTORIA JUNGFRAU GRAND HOTEL & SPA

Victoria Jungfrau Grand Hotel & Spa (Luxury): Feeling fancy? Then stay at the most beautiful and spectacular hotel in Interlaken! Victoria Jungfrau Big Hotel & Spa will make sure you can enjoy that big holiday you've been dreaming of.

Perched below the Jungfrau (Mt. Virgin) and between two popular lakes, this 5-star hotel wows its visitors with stunning mountain views of the Bernese Highlands. For me, one of the important aspects I consider when picking a place to base in is the right location with beautiful views, and having fast internet is a huge advantage since I'm working and traveling. This hotel is simply absolute perfection- with an on-point service and an indoor pool which is wonderful in the summer. The greatest location to stay in Interlaken if you are searching for luxury!

Address: Höheweg 41, 3800 Interlaken, Switzerland

Phone:+41 33 828 28 28

HOTEL INTERLAKEN

Hotel Interlaken (Luxury): Set amid Interlaken is the most popular hotel in the whole town—Hotel Interlaken. This 4-star hotel is the oldest in the neighborhood yet you don't be deceived by its outer aspect. The hotel boasts a combination of ancient and contemporary conveniences with big rooms, balconies overlooking the church and mountains, and a nice restaurant and bar to unwind after a day of trekking. There are numerous accommodations from single rooms to suites so you may have your solitude.

Even if it's a touch pricey, the breakfast is extremely wonderful here. They feature a gorgeous garden grass area with sun loungers if you wish to take advantage of the fresh air in the morning. The closeness to the Japanese Gardens, train stations, stores, and restaurants is a major benefit! Not inexpensive but when it comes to selecting the finest hotel to stay in Interlaken, trust Hotel Interlaken to make your visit genuinely distinctive and unforgettable!

Address: Höheweg 74, 3800 Interlaken, Switzerland

Phone: +41 33 826 68 68

HOTEL DU NORD

Hotel Du Nord (Luxury): Location-wise, Hotel Du Nord is by far one of the greatest hotels in Interlaken. It's just a stone's throw away from the rail station (Interlaken Ost and West station) which is a great starting place for exciting excursions into the Jungfrau area. You are not traveling to Switzerland if you can't locate a resort that gives beautiful views and Hotel Du Nord has it! I'd also rate the breakfast here as excellent!

Numerous alternatives will make your belly happy before you start your first trek of the day. Plus, the personnel makes a difference in your stay! They're incredibly helpful when it comes to proposing nice things to do in Interlaken. With recently refurbished accommodations, free use of bicycles, and complimentary parking, you can't look beyond Hotel Du Nord!

Address: Höheweg 70, 3800 Interlaken, Switzerland
Phone: +41 33 827 50 50

HOTEL BELLEVUE

Hotel Bellevue (Luxury): Hotel Bellevue is positioned right on the Aare River with a lovely mountain background. This small minimalist-style hotel is only a short walk to the train station, Interlaken museum, and the hustle and activity of Interlaken. It's a peaceful, secluded, and expensive resort with three kinds of accommodation-hotel rooms, flats, and a river home.

There are 38 stylish rooms furnished with comfy mattresses, hot tubs, and a charming workstation. The River House is great for a family escape with a huge garden directly on the river. On the topmost level, you'll discover big apartments that give a magnificent view of the river and the Alps.

Cleanliness and offering exceptional service are among the main goals of Hotel Bellevue so expect to enjoy a pleasant stay. Hands down! This is one of my favorite hotel

Address: Marktgasse 59, 3800 Interlaken, Switzerland

Phone:+41 33 822 44 31

4 Mid-Range Hotels In Interlaken

HOTEL ALPHORN

Not too elegant but Hotel Alphorn undoubtedly performs a terrific job in terms of satisfying their guests' requirements. This family-run hotel provides rooms furnished with flat-screen TVs but who wants to watch TV if you can enjoy the amazing views and paragliders flying over the river, valleys, and mountains? It's a walking distance of the West train station and the gorgeous river of Interlaken.

The location is wonderful and peaceful but still near enough to the markets, pubs, and restaurants which is excellent for tourists who don't want to stay in the core of the hectic city. The motel comes in quite helpful since they provide a storage area for mountain bikes and skis. For roughly $100, you can obtain a double room that includes a buffet breakfast. Without a doubt, this hotel provides value for money!

Address: Rothornstrasse 29A, 3800 Interlaken, Switzerland

Phone:+41 33 822 30 51

HIRSCHEN

Hirschen (Value): This chalet-style hotel has accommodations ranging from single to family rooms with a laid-back attitude making it a great option for solo, couple, and family tourists. Located centrally, it allows convenient access to everything in Interlaken. The property contains plenty of flowers and decorations, a garden patio, a wine cellar, and a kids' playground.

Although the hotel is not very huge, undoubtedly it's a wonderful selection for people who don't want to spend a lot on lodging in Interlaken. Besides, you may still revel in the magnificent view of mountains from the garden or in your apartment. I enjoy the breakfast better since they have too many selections and it's fairly delicious- enough to make your tummy happy! I strongly suggest this hotel!

Address: Hauptstrasse 11, 3800 Matten bei Interlaken, Switzerland

Phone: +41 33 822 15 45

NEUHAUS GOLF- & STRANDHOTEL

Neuhaus Golf- & Strandhotel (Value/Tranquility): If you seek a quick respite from the rush and bustle, this lakeside hotel could be your best alternative! Sure this hotel is not high-end but the views and surroundings are just beautiful enough that you can't say no to staying in this area. You may assume you'll become bored here but you're incorrect. There are lot of stuff to do here- from river cruises, golfing, kayaking, or paragliding. I appreciate the tranquil setting better, actually, you can rest more with stunning green sights around. Even if this hotel is out of the city, they provide a free shuttle service to Interlaken Center and the free parking is an added plus. Friendly, pleasant, and with a beautiful location, it is a hotel you cannot go wrong with.

Address: Seestrasse 119, 3800 Unterseen, Switzerland

Phone: +41 33 822 82 82

HOTEL BEAUSITE

Hotel Beausite (Excellent Host): Technically positioned right in the middle of Interlaken, Hotel Beausite is a family-run company and a well-maintained property with a green garden, terrace, and excellent views of the Alps. It is about a five-minute walk to Interlaken West Train Station.

And when it comes to lodging, the hotel boasts a nice selection of accommodations from a regular double room to a family room. Each room is provided with a coffee maker, ensuite bathroom, flat-screen TV, and floor-to-ceiling windows. The breakfast is lovely and each visitor may acquire a complimentary Interlaken card which allows free usage of public transit in the town. This hotel in Interlaken is quite renowned.

Address: Seestrasse 16, 3600 Thun, Switzerland

4 Cheap Hostels In Interlaken

BACKPACKERS VILLA SONNENHOF – HOSTEL INTERLAKEN

Backpackers Villa Sonnenhof - Hostel Interlaken (Budget): (I stayed there) Okay, here's the good news: The greatest hostel in Switzerland is in Interlaken and that's no other than

Backpackpackers Villa. If you're searching for a quiet hostel where you can work on your laptop comfortably and save your cash at the same time, this is the spot!

It's positioned between the two rail terminals which gives it an ideal spot to base for exploring outside. Imagine waking up with Mt. Virgin view if you get the Jungfrau accommodation. Some of the amenities you may enjoy whilst staying here include the buffet breakfast, bedsheets, and towels, lockers, 24-hour kitchen use, fast internet, entrance to public indoor and outdoor pools, mini-golf, and tennis. No surprise why Backpackers Villa ranked best!

Address: Alpenstrasse 16, 3800 Interlaken, Switzerland
Phone: +41 33 826 71 71

HAPPY INN LODGE

Happy Inn Lodge (Budget): The Happy Inn Lodge provides budget-saving cozy accommodations with many bunk beds in the middle of Interlaken. Perfect for lone travelers and couples traveling on a tight budget, room costs vary from $23 (6-bed dorm rooms with shared bathroom) to $72 (twin rooms with private shower) furnished with a sink, closet, and mirror inside.

Although the hostel is quite basic, it includes everything you need from hot showers to entertainment and the fact that staff can plan events for you is an added plus! While in the summer you may rent a private vehicle or a bike, a free shuttle to the nearest ski stations is available in the winter. I particularly adore the sociable ambiance of this hostel-style inn whereby you can easily get food and drink in the cozy bar and restaurant or on the terrace outdoors.

Address: Rosenstrasse 17, 3800 Interlaken, Switzerland

Phone: +41 33 822 32 25

INTERLAKEN YOUTH HOSTEL

Interlaken Youth Hostel (Budget/Bestseller): Are you searching for a top-rated and immaculate hostel while traveling in Interlaken? Then look no more and check out Interlaken Youth Hostel. This youth hostel is more like a hotel and it's in a wonderful position since it's directly adjacent to the train station and between two lakes.

Perfect for lone travelers or families, Interlaken Youth Hostel features a range of accommodation choices from a private single room, or family room to a dorm room that fits up to 4 people. Plus visitors may hire bikes, play billiards, or join a game of ping pong - I think you'll have a lot of fun here. For travelers, the Interlaken Youth Hostel can be excellent.

Address: Untere Bönigstrasse 3a, 3800 Interlaken, Switzerland

Phone: +41 33 826 10 90

BALMERS BACKPACKERS HOSTEL

Balmers Backpackers Hostel (Budget/Party): From the name itself Balmers Hostel is a nexus for predominantly young travelers from across the globe. If you're a party lover or want to make friends, then Balmers is undoubtedly the finest cheap hostel for you. The venue recalls Mad Monkey Hostels in Asia where visitors may interact and party with live music— simply grab a drink and

INTERLAKEN TRAVEL GUIDE 2024

enjoy the music! The hostel hosts events throughout the summer months.

They also give free bicycles and there's a garden with hammocks, BBQ amenities, and nice communal rooms. You may either stay in a room or glamping that can fit up to 6 people. Well, whether you travel there in the summer or in the winter, this hostel provides loads of things. This is highly recommended for single travelers!

Address: Hauptstrasse 23, 3800 Matten bei Interlaken, Switzerland

Phone: +41 33 822 19 61

Chapter 4

Exploring Interlaken - 20 Mind-blowing Things to do in Interlaken (Top Attractions, and Fun Outdoor Activities)

1. Explore the St. Beatus Caves

One of the unusual must-visit attractions to see in Interlaken is the St. Beatus Caves. Located only a few minutes away from Interlaken, the caverns are a fantastic location for nature lovers and adventure enthusiasts alike.

The St. Beatus caverns are a network of subterranean caverns that were created millions of years ago.

Named for St. Beatus, a Christian hermit who is claimed to have resided in the caverns around the sixth century, I think the famous caves are one of Switzerland's best-kept secrets.

Visitors to the St. Beatus caverns may explore the caverns on a guided tour, experiencing a network of subterranean chambers and passages.

Each has its distinctive rock formations, stalactites, and stalagmites. The trip is supervised by qualified experts who give extensive information about the history and geology of the caverns.

For me, the highlight of the excursion is the subterranean waterfall. Located deep within the caverns, it's a stunning site to witness.

- Good to know: The St. Beatus Caves also contain a museum that shows the rich history and culture of the area, with a variety of antiquities and exhibits. I believe a visit to this hidden treasure is one of the nicest things to do in Interlaken.

- Opening times: Late March to mid-November: every day from 09:00 –

18:00; on Fridays and Saturdays, open until 21:00.

- Price:Adults can enter for CHF 19, or CHF 17 with a Berner-Oberland Visitors Card, while children between six and sixteen can enter for CHF 11, or CHF 10 with the Berner-Oberland Visitors Card.

  Family pass involving parents or grandparents (maximum two persons) and their children/grandchildren between ages 6-16: CHF 49

  Dogs: CHF 10

- Address: Staatsstrasse 30, 3800 Sundlauenen, Switzerland

- Phone:+41 33 841 16 43

2. Harder Kulm

After completing the trek to Interlaken, stretch your legs out on the Harder—a 1,322-meter peak that overlooks the resort town and its dazzling lakes.

It's possible to walk to the peak by a difficult trail from the Harderbahn station, but unless you're an enthusiastic trekker, you may be better off conserving your energy and whizzing to the Harder Kulm station on a century-old funicular in only 10 minutes. The near-vertical railway gradient will make you grateful you took the trip instead of hoofing up on foot.

From there, you may start your stroll on a short, uphill brick road with great views of the countryside. It's impossible not to grin when you see the funny wooden sculptures of people yodeling in traditional mountain clothing and waving the red-and-white Swiss flags that line the path. Plus, they make postcard-worthy picture subjects.

At the end of the brick walk, head right to begin the Harder Kulm Circular walk. The hour-long journey leads you through a dark mountain forest, where morning mist floating over the moss and leaves create a lovely environment. The route ultimately opens up to a panoramic vista of Lake Brienz, Lake Thun, and the Alps, before guiding you back to the trailhead. It's the ideal introduction to the "Adventure Capital of Europe."

It's ideal to do the climb immediately before midday since the route drops you off directly in front of the castle-like Harder Kulm Panorama Restaurant, featuring cheese fondue, potato rosti, grilled meats, and traditional Alpine macaroni.

From here, you can also stand atop the Zwei-Seen-Steg (Two Lakes Bridge) observation platform and capture the ultimate Interlaken selfie. Don't just watch out, though—look down as well. The glass-bottomed floor will offer you another viewpoint of the waters below.

Want to view some of the local creatures that call this terrain their home? Swing by the Alpine Wildlife Park at the foot of their Harderbahn. The free zoo allows travelers the opportunity to come up close to majestic ibex and cuddly marmots.

Address: 3800 Unterseen, Switzerland

3. Höhematte Park & the Höheweg

An area of 14 hectares in the center of Interlaken that belonged to the Augustinian monastery was bought in 1860 by a consortium of 37 hotel owners and private residents to be left as an open space, a unique example of foreseeing urban planning.

Through its length runs the Höheweg, a wonderful road connecting the east and west train stations that gives a spectacular view of the Jungfrau, flanked by hotels and flower gardens. Alongside it lies the Kursaal, with a theater, a café, and lovely gardens with a floral clock, as well as several hotels, including the 150-year-old Victoria Jungfrau Hotel, itself a local icon.

Next to the Hotel Interlaken, you'll discover the modest Garden of Friendship, the first Japanese garden in Switzerland, a calm location with floral plants, water, and koi fish. The garden was a present from Ōtsu, Interlaken's sister city in Japan.

The park is the favorite landing location for hang gliders—one of the most popular of the various experiences you can enjoy in Interlaken. For the less courageous, horse-drawn carriages park along the street in front of the park.

In the winter, the Höhematte turns into Ice Magic, with five rinks linked by ice ramps. Rinks are for all levels of skater, with an ice-skating rink that's suitable for beginners, but with enough room for faster skaters and a curling rink where you can try your hand at this activity that's quite popular in Switzerland.

Address:3800 Interlaken, Switzerland

4. Reach new heights at Rope Park Interlaken

- Prices:
- Adults: CHF 42
- Children under 16: CHF 31

- Groups of 10 or more: CHF 38

If you have a taste for adventure and adrenaline-fuelled activities, I'd suggest taking a trip to Rope Park Interlaken.

Amid scenic Interlaken, this park provides a truly thrilling chance to test your talents and conquer your anxieties.

Rope Park Interlaken offers numerous courses of differing difficulty levels. Soar far above the earth with this family-friendly adventure in Interlaken.

The courses are meant to test your balance, agility, and strength, and contain a range of demanding obstacles such as zip lines, rope bridges, and swinging logs up to 20 meters in the air.

Good to know: The park is excellent for both youngsters and adults.

Address: Wagnerenstrasse, 3800 Interlaken, Switzerland

Phone: +41 33 224 07 07

5. Take the train to Schynige Platte

- Prices: From CHF 32

Schynige Platte is a mountain ridge found in the world-famous Bernese Oberland area of Switzerland.

INTERLAKEN TRAVEL GUIDE 2024

I believe this is a genuine bucket list destination for nature lovers and hikers, and one of the finest ways to reach the summit of the mountain is by riding the cogwheel train from Wilderswil.

The train trip to Schynige Platte provides beautiful views of the surrounding mountains, valleys, and lakes.

You'll travel through fertile meadows, deep woods, and high cliffs, making it a fascinating ride to the top which rises at 1,967 meters.

Once you reach the summit, you will be rewarded with awe-inspiring panoramic views of the Swiss Alps, including the Eiger, Mönch, and Jungfrau mountains.

Various hiking paths start from the peak, ranging from short hikes to strenuous expeditions.

I'd also suggest visiting the Alpine Garden situated at the summit, which shows over 750 varieties of flora endemic to the Swiss Alps.

Hike the Schynige Platte Trails

From Wilderswil, a five-minute walk from the Interlaken Ost train station, you can take a rack-railroad that has been taking sightseers up to the Schynige Platte—a mountain slope that gets its name from its reflected wall of slate—since it opened in 1893. The hour-long journey is a sequence of ever-changing Alpine landscapes, and at the summit, you'll discover one of the greatest panoramic views of the Alps, covering the Eiger, Mönch, and Jungfrau peaks as well as Lake Thun.

The vistas are much greater than the paths that begin at the summit. The simplest of them, with a sequence of superb vistas, is the 45-minute climb to the Daube Viewpoint. Lake Thun is far below, encircled by snowcapped hills. Take a picnic and relish the occasion before finishing the remainder of the circle, taking you back to the Schynige Platte station.

The Oberburghorn Trail extends from the Daube Viewpoint, forming an even longer -- around three-kilometer - circle over a mountain crest with 360-degree views. This easy-to-moderate path is very flat, and the vistas are much nicer than the shorter circle. There's a long wooden stairway to the lookout at the very top, definitely worth the walk. A third circle, the Loucherhorn Trail, adds around three kilometers and additional vistas, looping a little lower past verdant Alpine meadows with grazing Brown Swiss cows.

Near the station is a lovely Alpine Botanic Garden, with 600 varieties of flowers and other plants that can live and grow in this high-altitude environment. It puts 720 unique plants on exhibit in 16 diverse environments, ranging from lime-free soils and windy corners to small icy valleys. If you're fortunate there may be locals playing traditional Swiss Alphorns at the Schynige Platte station.

Good to know: After reaching the summit, I'd suggest eating lunch at the Schynige Platte Restaurant, which provides exquisite traditional Swiss food with spectacular views of the Alps.

Address: 3815 Gsteigwiler, Switzerland

6. Visit the medieval town of Unterseen

Unterseen is a wonderful ancient village situated roughly a 20-minute walk from Interlaken. The small village is located on the banks of the Aare River and is surrounded by stunning mountain panoramas and pure natural beauty.

Here, I'd suggest having a leisurely walk around the town's meandering alleyways, admiring the lovely architecture, and browsing the local stores and cafés for real Swiss food and handicrafts.

One of the attractions of a visit to Unterseen is the remains of Unterseen Castle. This majestic castle dates back to the 13th century and is a recognized Swiss historic monument of national importance.

For tourists who enjoy taking part in outdoor sports, Unterseen provides lots of chances for hiking and cycling.

The Aare River is a favorite site among residents for both swimming and kayaking. Here, you may also enjoy a lovely boat trip down the river to completely take in the mountain scenery.

Good to know: Another must-see sight in Unterseen is the St. Nicholas Church. This lovely church dates back to the 15th century and is famed for its gorgeous stained glass windows and elaborate wood decorations.

The Marktgasse goes northwest from the Interlaken post office and over the Spielmatten islands and the river to the modest hamlet of Unterseen, at the foot of Mt. Harder. This is one of the numerous settlements that constitute Interlaken, and in this historic section of town stands the 1471 parish church, featuring a Late Gothic tower.

In this area, you'll discover some gorgeous wooden chalets of the type you'd expect to see in little mountain towns, not in a bustling resort hub like Interlaken. Set amid verdant gardens, they may even have farm animals grazing on the lawns. Small eateries surrounding the picturesque Stadthausplatz provide typical Swiss meals.

Address:3800, Switzerland

7. Cross the Panoramabrücke Sigriswil (Sigriswil Panorama Bridge)

The vista down into the Gummischlucht canyon, 182 meters (600 feet) below, as you cross the new suspension footbridge is one you won't forget. The bridge over Lake Thun is 330 meters (more than 1,000 feet) long and is one of three suspension bridges on the famous Lake Thun Panoramic Circular Trail linking mountain and coastline pathways around the lake.

Panoramic views from the bridge and path include the Eiger, Mönch, and Jungfrau, and neighboring peaks of the Bernese Alps. The towns of Sigriswil and Aeschlen, at each end of the suspension bridge, are also wonderful locations to explore, as well.

There's a nice farm stand just across the river in Sigriswil, where you can pick up local delicacies and fresh veggies for a picnic.

Address: Raftstrasse 31-33, 3655 Sigriswil, Switzerland

8. Paragliding

You won't be in Interlaken long before you'll see the bright-colored parachutes of paragliders in the sky or landing at Höhematte Park. Flying through the Alpine air with a 360-degree vista of the snow-covered Alps above the lakes and beautiful green meadows is an incredible experience. It's no surprise it is one of the most popular things to do in Interlaken.

You'll have your pick of numerous paragliding outfitters, and if this is your first flight, you will be matched with an experienced guide. Try a Tandem Paragliding Experience from Interlaken. Taking to the air is simple: from a steep slope, you just sprint downward until the wind lifts you off the earth. The mountains are all around, and Interlaken extends below as you glide.

Those who like their aerial experiences a bit closer to the ground will discover thrills at Interlaken Ropes Park, where zip lines, swings, wooden bridges, and rope courses offer fun for families in a woodland environment.

Good to know: If you're vulnerable to motion sickness, it's worth understanding that paragliding may provoke it. I learned this the hard way!

9. Swiss Open-Air Museum Ballenberg

A 20-minute drive or 40-minute train trip from Interlaken is one of Europe's greatest living history museums. Ballenberg spans over 124 acres of alpine terrain in several hamlet and farmhouse groupings depicting various Swiss regions and their traditional ways of life.

Historic homes, barns, stores, and other structures were relocated here from their original places, with their furniture, decorations, utensils, and equipment. Old crafts and old rituals are recreated here, and on a visit, you may witness anything from woodcarving and cooperage to lace- and cheese-making demonstrations.

The residences reflect various types from the most humble cabins and rustic farmhouses to magnificent dwellings of the well-to-do, but the emphasis is on how people lived, how they created their commodities, and how they traded and shared within their communities. Special displays may cover one component of lifein depth, such as child labor on farms or a specific skill and its growth.

You could easily spend an entire day exploring all the buildings and exhibits on this interesting trip back in time. Ask the Interlaken Tourist Office for information on packages that include boat and bus travel from Interlaken to Ballenberg.

Address: Museumsstrasse 131, Hofstetten bei Brienz

10. Experience Lake Brienz by boat

I believe that one of the greatest ways to experience the beautiful natural beauty of Interlaken is to take a boat trip on Lake Brienz.

With its crystal-clear blue waters and magnificent mountain panoramas, Lake Brienz is a must-visit site for anybody going to Interlaken.

There are various boat cruises offered that provide varied experiences for guests.

My favorite choice is the historic paddle steamer boat excursion, which takes you on a leisurely cruise around the lake, affording amazing vistas of the surrounding mountains and woods.

For those searching for a more daring experience, I'd also suggest a speedboat trip, which provides a thrilling journey over the lake at high speeds.

These trips are excellent for adrenaline freaks like me who adore the feeling of wind rushing through your hair as you race over the ocean.

No matter whatever style of boat cruise you pick, Lake Brienz is a genuine jewel of Interlaken. From the serene seas to the breathtaking mountains, going to the water is one of the nicest things to do in Interlaken.

Good to know: You may also opt to hire your boats and explore the lake at your speed. I believe this is a terrific alternative for families or groups of friends who wish to have a more calm time on the lake.

11. Cruise on Lake Thun

Lake Thun is certainly one of the most beautiful lakes in Switzerland. It is bordered by the gorgeous Swiss Alps, and it provides a broad selection of water sports that both residents and visitors alike may enjoy.

You may take a boat trip on the lake and enjoy the spectacular views of the surrounding mountain landscape. The boat trip runs for around two hours, and it includes stops at several areas of interest along the route.

There are also private boat trips available, which I'd suggest for individuals who like a more personal and customized experience.

For individuals who prefer to be active, Lake Thun provides a range of water activities like as kayaking, paddleboarding, and windsurfing.

There are various rental businesses placed around the lake where tourists may rent equipment and take instruction if required.

Insider travel tip: Fishing aficionados may also enjoy the lake's large fish population. You may get a fishing permit and enjoy a quiet day fishing on the lake.

12. Tour the gorgeous Blue Lake & Öschinen Lake

One of the nicest things to do in Interlaken – and a particular favorite of mine – is to visit the lovely Blue Lake and Öschinen Lake.

The Blue Lake, also known as Blausee, is a crystal blue lake surrounded by lush green woods and mountains, situated only a few miles from Interlaken.

Öschinen Lake is another lovely lake found in the famed Bernese Oberland area of Switzerland.

Surrounded by snow-capped mountains and fed by massive glaciers, it is a popular destination for hiking, skiing, and other outdoor activities among visitors and residents alike.

Both Blue Lake and Öschinen Lake provide a serenely tranquil atmosphere, excellent for people who wish to escape the hustle and bustle of daily life and rest.

You may enjoy the wonderful views, take a plunge in the cold waters, or just sit back and relax in the gorgeous surroundings.

13. **Go white water rafting on Lütschine River**

The Lütschine River is a famous place for white water rafting due to its fast-flowing rapids and spectacular surroundings.

While white water rafting on the Lütschine River is not reserved for experienced rafters, notice that you do need to be a very good swimmer to participate.

The river is separated into numerous portions, each with increasing degrees of difficulty. Rafting tours normally last for roughly two to three hours in the grades three and four rapids.

The drive takes you through magnificent landscapes and gives amazing views of the neighboring mountains.

White water rafting on the Lütschine River is an exciting sport that I know will get your heart pounding and kindle your adventurous spirit!

Good to know: The minimum age requirement is normally 14 years of age, and participants must be able to swim. Don't forget to bring a change of clothing for afterward!

Address: 3818 Grindelwald, Switzerland

14. Explore the Weissenau Nature Reserve

The Weissenau Nature Reserve is a lovely natural area situated on the shores of Lake Thun near Interlaken, Switzerland. Nature lovers and outdoor aficionados, I've included this one for you!

Choose to explore the reserve on foot, by bike, or on horseback.

Various routes snake through the reserve, affording wonderful views of the surrounding mountains and valleys. The paths are well-marked and vary in difficulty from simple to moderate.

One of the features of the Weissenau Nature Reserve is the Weissenau Castle remains.

At the summit, you may walk out onto a snowy expanse more than 3,450 meters above sea level and stare out at the majestic Swiss Alps and the Aletsch Glacier, just as passengers have done since the train station opened in 1912.

Between the thin air and the awe-striking panoramas, it's a disorienting experience that will remain with you. Make sure to explore other activities at the Jungfraujoch, such as wandering through the Ice Palace, where the entire floor is frozenfrom floor to ceiling, adorned with intricate ice sculptures. Additionally, delve into the museum-like exhibitions detailing how miners constructed this railway over a century ago using basic handheld tools.

Address: Weissenaustrasse, 3800 Unterseen, Switzerland

15. Go skiing in the Jungfrau Ski Region

Interlaken is just a winter paradise, and skiing in the Jungfrau Ski Region is one of the finest things to do while you're there. Many individuals travel expressly for that purpose.

The area boasts three top-tier ski resorts: Grindelwald-First, Kleine Scheidegg-Männlichen, and Mürren-Schilthorn.

With almost 200 km of pistes, I enjoy that the Jungfrau Ski Region is suited for skiers of all abilities.

You'll be delighted to find that the ski lifts in the Jungfrau Ski Region are contemporary and efficient

– and there are enough of them – so you won't have to wait long to get to the top of the mountain.

If you're a novice, various ski schools in the Jungfrau Ski Region provide instruction for all ages and abilities.

The instructors are educated and gentle, and they'll help you grow your confidence on the slopes and move up to solo skis. Discover more of the top ski resorts for novices in my guide.

Good to know: If skiing isn't your thing, there are plenty of other winter sports to enjoy in the Jungfrau Ski Region, including snowshoeing, ice skating, and tobogganing.

Address: Grundstrasse 54, 3818 Grindelwald, Switzerland

16. Check out the Interlaken Castle and Monastery.

The Interlaken Monastery and Castle is not just for those who are interested in architecture and history for the most part. It is, in my opinion, an excellent location to have the opportunity to explore the culture and beauty of the Swiss town.

A magnificent example of medieval Swiss architecture, the castle was built in the 12th century and dates back to that period. One of the most enjoyable things to do in Interlaken is to pay a visit to the city. This will allow you to experience history.

The monastic structure, on the other hand, is a magnificent example of the Baroque architectural style and was constructed in the 18th century.

The abbey and castle, which have been classified as Swiss Heritage Sites of National Significance, are a picture of the past that preserves the genuine Swiss culture of days gone by.

An insider travel tip: From the tower of the castle, you can take in breathtaking vistas of the town and the mountains that surround it for an unforgettable experience. In addition, I would suggest that you have a picnic in the garden of the monastery since it is a great location to relax and take in the breathtaking views.

Address: Schloss 1, 3800 Interlaken, Switzerland

17.   Get familiar with the hiking paths.

Interlaken is a veritable paradise for hikers; its breathtaking natural surroundings and vast network of hiking routes astound even seasoned hikers. Whether you're an expert hiker or a total novice, there is a route for everyone.

My favorite hiking track in Interlaken is the Eiger track which gives amazing views of the Eiger, Mönch, and Jungfrau mountains.

The path is roughly seven miles long and takes around two to three hours to complete. While it is a difficult trek with some steep portions, the sights are worth the effort if you're able to.

If you're wanting a hard trek, I'd suggest the Hardergrat Trail for you. This trek is regarded as one of the most beautiful but demanding (and perhaps deadly) walks in Switzerland.

The path is around 24 km long and takes about 12 to 14 hours to finish. Much of this path is on clearly defined ridges, making it problematic for certain walkers.

Good to know: Other popular hiking paths are the Lake Brienz Trail and Schynige Platte Trail which provide similarly beautiful vistas.

18. Have a canyoning experience

Perfect for adrenaline addicts, canyoning in Interlaken is an exciting experience paired with stunning scenery.

It's a thrilling experience that mixes a passion for adventure with the immense natural beauty of Interlaken and the neighboring villages.

Various canyoning firms in Interlaken provide guided trips for all ability levels, from total novices to seasoned experts.

They supply all the essential equipment and safety gear, including wetsuits, helmets, and harnesses. The guides are well-educated and experienced, ensuring a safe and fun experience for everyone.

One of the most popular canyoning routes that I'd suggest is the Chli Schlieren Canyon, which has a succession of exciting leaps, slides, and abseils. It's a hard journey that needs some physical fitness and a spirit of adventure.

Another alternative is the Grimsel Canyon, which is excellent for novices and provides a more calm experience.

Good to know: It's vital to note that canyoning may be a highly hazardous sport if not done correctly. Always pick a trustworthy business with competent guides and follow their directions attentively.

19. Take a journey to Giessbach Falls

Giessbach Falls is a high waterfall found in Interlaken. It's surrounded by breathtaking landscapes, including lush green woods and dramatic mountain vistas you won't find anywhere else.

To get to Giessbach Falls, you may take a boat from Interlaken to the town of Brienz. From there, a funicular train brings you up to the falls.

I'd suggest going after the snow has melted in spring since this will give the strongest water flow.

Once reaching the falls, you may take a short trek to the top for an even greater view of the flowing water. The waterfall plunges over 400 meters, giving it a real sight.

Good to know: You may also marvel at Giessbach Falls from on the water with a jetboat excursion on Lake Brienz.

Address: 3855 Brienz, Switzerland

20. See the remains of Unspunnen Castle

The ruined castle is situated on a hill in the Bernese area of Wilderswil overlooking Interlaken and is readily accessible by a short trek. The castle dates back to the early 12th century and was once a strong fortification.

Since 1805, the site has been the setting of the annual Unspunnen festival (Unspunnenfest) — a celebration of traditional Swiss contests conducted in the fields below the ruins about every 12 years.

Here, you may explore the ruins and take a trip back in time while you marvel at the views of Interlaken and the surrounding countryside.

The castle grounds are well-maintained, so I'd suggest bringing over a picnic to eat while taking in the sights.

Good to know: The remains of Unspunnen Castle are a favorite destination for keen photographers. The castle's position on a hill gives a stunning background for photography, and the ruins themselves make for a fascinating subject.

Address: Burgenweg, 3812 Wilderswil, Switzerland

Chapter 5

Day Trips from Interlaken

Lauterbrunnen

To sum Lauterbrunnen up in a word would be hard since there are so many amazing things about it.

Charming Swiss chalet structures, stunning waterfalls, first-class restaurants, and walks that will take you across the wonderful Swiss landscape are just the beginning.

Lauterbrunnen is an excellent day excursion from Interlaken and one of the greatest sites to see the other stunning tiny towns and villages in the Jungfrau area.

By rail from Interlaken, hourly trains leave from Interlaken East Train Station. Taking the 20-minute excursion by rail to Lauterbrunnen is quite simple

Murren

The little cliff-side, car-free town of Murren is a vision of fairytale Switzerland in all its beauty. It can be accessed by cable car from Lauterbrunnen and is one of the top trekking sites in the Alps. Wander along pathways through Swiss floral meadows and listen out for the sound of the cowbells ringing as the cows graze on the hillside.

Once at Murren, the Northface Trail provides keen hikers the possibility to explore the region.
In just five minutes, a funicular train departing from Murren will transport you to the summit of Allmendhubel. Here you will discover the floral

walking route and a café affording uninterrupted views of the Eiger, Mönch, and Jungfrau mountains. There are various walks through the spectacular alpine environment, including a hiking track that climbs up to the Schilthorn.

Shilthorn

Schilthorn is home to the Piz Gloria viewpoint and, at 2,960 meters, is one of the greatest views accessible by cable car from Lauterbrunnen or Murren. It is fondly known as the "007 viewpoint" because the James Bond film "On Her Majesty's Service" was shot here.

At the top of the mountain, you will discover a restaurant. Time a visit at sunset for arguably the most beautiful views of the Swiss skyline that you could imagine.

Grindelwald

No surprise that Grindelwald is another gorgeous Swiss town high on the list of day excursions from Interlaken. From the main town of Grindelwald, you may visit the Gletscherschlucht, a beautiful glacial canyon, or the hypnotic alpine lake of Bachalpsee.

One of the most popular attractions in Grindelwald is riding the cable car to Mount First Cliff Walk (also known as Skywalk Grindelwald).

The boardwalk hangs over the edge of the mountain giving for beautiful, if not a bit dangerous, vistas!

For additional adrenaline sports in Grindelwald, try the sky gliders, canyon swing, mountain carts, and skiing in winter.

A 45-minute direct train from Ost station to Grindelwald will bring you to an alpine wonderland.

Jungfraujoch - The Top of Europe

The most popular day excursion from Interlaken is to take a journey on the cogwheel train up to Jungfraujoch, Europe's highest-altitude railway station.

The trip takes one and a half hours from the station at Lauterbrunnen, with a break in Kleine Scheidegg.

From the time you climb onboard this lovely method of conveyance, the sights are amazing as it gradually begins its way to the top of the mountain. It is best to come early to do this journey since there are various things to try out at the summit of Jungfraujoch.

With snow at the peak, it's hard to imagine the valley below is swathed in sunlight and verdant fields. Oh, and did I mention it is a Unesco World Heritage Site?

Kleine Scheidegg

Kleine Scheidegg railway sits on the slopes of the Eiger - the most hazardous mountain in the world.
It is the midway station for day trip guests coming to Jungfraujoch by rail and offers various locations to get a bite to eat and drink before continuing up the mountain.

Kleine Scheidegg also offers guests some good alpine walking routes to explore with beautiful views over the Bernese Oberland mountains.

Schynige Platte

Schynige Platte is one of the most accessible mountain destinations in the Jungfrau range from Interlaken. It is lesser known than Jungfraujoch or

Lauterbrunnen, and therefore it is a calm spot to explore.

Like the gorgeous alpine train trip to Kleine Scheidegg, this hour-long trek up the mountain is a terrific experience.

Step out at the summit and proceed to the floral alpine gardens for amazing views of the surrounding area. The train up to Schynige Platte leaves at Wilderswill, which may be accessed by vehicle or rail from Interlaken.

If you come in the summer season, you will surely hear the sounds of the alphorn players who delight guests with sounds from these historic Swiss instruments. Afterward, venture out on the 4-mile Panorama loop route to discover why Switzerland is one of the most beautiful destinations in Europe.

Chapter 6

Dining in Interlaken

Top local food in Interlaken

- **Fondue Bourguignonne:** A version of fondue where bite-sized chunks of beef are fried in hot oil and then dipped into different sauces.

- **Swiss-style Ravioli**: Homemade pasta pockets filled with cheese, spinach, or meat, served with a creamy sauce or tomato ragu.

- **Swiss Alpine Soup:** A substantial soup created with locally obtained ingredients such as root vegetables, barley, and bits of meat, excellent for warming up after a day of sightseeing.

- **Zuger Kirschtorte**: A typical Swiss cherry liqueur-infused cake filled with cream and topped with chocolate shavings, a delectable delicacy to enjoy with a cup of coffee.

- **Bernese Gingerbread**: Spiced gingerbread cookies prepared with honey, almonds, and a combination of toasty spices, a delicious delicacy to enjoy with a glass of mulled wine during the Christmas season.

- **Rösti**: Crispy grated potatoes eaten as a side dish or topped with cheese, bacon, or fried eggs.

- **Cheese Fondue**: A rich and creamy melted cheese dip served with bread pieces for dipping.

- **Raclette**: Melted cheese scraped over potatoes, bread, or vegetables, frequently accompanied with pickles and onions.

- **Älplermagronen**: A substantial Alpine meal including pasta, potatoes, cheese, and caramelized onions.

- **Swiss Chocolate**: Indulge in Switzerland's world-famous chocolate, available in numerous forms and tastes.

- **Berner Platte:** A classic Swiss meat plate with a range of cured meats, sausages, and smoked ham.

- **Birchermüesli**: A Swiss-style muesli prepared with oats, fruits, nuts, and yogurt or milk, excellent for breakfast or as a nutritious snack.

- **Zürcher Geschnetzeltes**: Sliced veal cooked in a creamy mushroom sauce, generally eaten over Rösti or noodles.

- **Swiss Alps Beer**: Sample locally made beers, ranging from light and refreshing to deep and malty, great for complementing with Swiss food.

- **Engadiner Nusstorte**: A wonderful nut-filled dessert created with caramelized sugar, nuts, and buttery dough, excellent for fulfilling your sweet craving.

Top Restaurants in Interlaken

Interlaken is a wonderful tourist resort nestled in the middle of Switzerland. While there are many things to do and see in the region, one of the most significant components of any trip experience is the cuisine. Interlaken boasts great restaurants that provide traditional Swiss cuisine, as well as other specialties.

Alpenblick Restaurant

If you're searching for a typical Swiss dining experience, then Alpenblick Restaurant is a must-visit. This charming chalet and restaurant has been serving traditional Swiss food for over 100 years and has been operated by the same husband and wife combination since 1980. It's situated in the charming village of Beatenberg, only a short drive from Interlaken. The menu features refined Swiss specialties including cheese fondue, rosti, and schnitzel, as well as a range of meats and seafood.

Address: Ägerten 1078A, 3825 Mürren, Switzerland

Phone: +41 33 855 13 27

Restaurant Taverne

Interlakenstrasse

Restaurant Taverne is a delightful family-operated Swiss restaurant situated in the town of Matten bei Interlaken. The menu contains a selection of classic

Swiss meals, including raclette, fondue, and different meat dishes.

The chef-recommended entrée is their slow-cooked pork belly, which is accompanied by smoky honey marinade, pumpkin puree, roasted potatoes, and romano beans. If you choose the Alpen cheese fondue, it is served with a delectable assortment of bread, baked potatoes, and pickles.

Address: Höheweg 74, 3800 Interlaken, Switzerland

Phone: +41 33 826 68 68

Grand Cafe Restaurant Schuh Hauptstrasse

Restaurant Schuh is another fantastic choice for authentic Swiss food. Luxurious and beautiful, it features a magnificent patio for the warmer months.

The restaurant is in the picturesque town of Unterseen, only a short walk from Interlaken.

The menu contains typical Swiss delicacies including rosti, cheese fondue, and other meat dishes. Everything here has been created using fresh and local ingredients.

Make sure you leave space for dessert — they are famed for their specialty chocolate and pastries, which you can also purchase at the next store.

Address: Höheweg 56, 3800 Interlaken, Switzerland

Phone:+41 33 888 80 50

Pizzeria Horn Höheweg

Pizzeria Horn is a casual restaurant situated in the middle of Interlaken. The restaurant delivers traditional Italian pizza created with fresh and high-quality ingredients. The menu also contains a selection of other Italian foods, such as pasta and antipasti.

Address: Harderstrasse 35, 3800 Interlaken, Switzerland

Restaurant Des Alpes

Restaurant Des Alpes is another fantastic choice for foreign food. The restaurant provides a selection of foods from diverse corners of the globe, including Asian, Italian, and Swiss cuisine. The menu includes staples like pizza and spaghetti, as well as local delicacies like rosti and cheese fondue.

Address: Höheweg 115, 3800 Interlaken, Switzerland

Phone: +41 33 828 81 81

La Terrasse

If you're searching for a good dining experience, then Restaurant La Terrasse, housed in Victoria Jungfrau Grand Hotel & Spa, is a superb option and has been lauded by the Michelin Guide. The restaurant is in the picturesque town of Wengen, a short train trip from Interlaken. The menu provides a choice of gourmet meals produced using local and seasonal ingredients. You'll discover lots of meat and seafood meals, as well as vegetarian alternatives. The restaurant also features a comprehensive wine selection covering local and foreign wines.

Address: Höheweg 41, 3800 Interlaken, Switzerland

Phone: +41 33 828 26 41

Hüsi Bierhaus Obere Gasse

Restaurant Hüsi Bierhaus is a budget-friendly alternative for eating in Interlaken. The restaurant provides a variety of foods, including burgers, salads, and pasta, as well as Swiss favorites like rosti and cheese fondue. The restaurant also offers a wonderful assortment of local and foreign beers.

They offer a beautiful view of the Alps and have a pleasant interior that makes you feel at home.

Address: **Postgasse 3, 3800 Interlaken, Switzerland**

Little Thai

Little Thai is a tiny restaurant providing wonderful Asian cuisine. Some of their greatest include spring rolls, papaya salad, pad thai, and Thai curries. If you don't like Thai, they also offer a few German, American, and Japanese items on the menu.

They offer a nice choice of craft beers to drink with your meal.

Address: Hauptstrasse 19, 3800 Matten bei Interlaken, Switzerland

Phone: +41 33 821 10 17

Aare Korean BBQ Restaurant

This Korean BBQ place is one of the top eateries in Interlaken. You may enjoy all the major hits of Korean cuisine, including Bulgogi, Japchae, and Bibimbap. There's a great view of Jungfrau and the Aare River from the café.

Address: Strandbadstrasse 15, 3800 Interlaken, Switzerland

Phone: +41 33 822 88 88

Restaurant Flamenco Interlaken

If you're in the mood for some distinct European cuisine, come to Flamenco for tapas — Spanish-style meat and seafood. Everything is freshly made and they feature frequent live music, so you're in for a night of enjoyment. The concept here is that you order a choice of tiny tapas items to split among your company, preferably accompanied by a bottle of wine!

Address: Blumenstrasse 16, 3800 Interlaken, Switzerland

Phone: +41 77 224 55 99

Chapter 7

Shopping areas in Interlaken

The top shopping alternatives in Interlaken

What are the greatest Interlaken markets and shopping locations in the city? We answer this question via our subject to get to know the greatest locations to shop in Interlaken, namely:

Migros

It is one of the greatest markets for Interlaken, which is a giant supermarket that gives vast alternatives for shopping, as it comprises more than 90 stores providing food in all its forms, in addition to many items and daily essentials, as well as a movie and other meals.

Address: Rugenparkstrasse 1, 3800 Interlaken, Switzerland

Coop Center

The Coop supermarket is one of the main Interlaken markets for foodstuffs, since it comprises food, fast food, and many daily essentials, the market gives continual offers and its prices are deemed pretty reasonable.

Address: Untere Bönigstrasse 5, 3800 Interlaken, Switzerland

Cajdrande Gallery du Lac

Such a business at the Grand Gallery du Lac Casagrande Galerie du Lac is one of the most popular shopping places in Interlaken where you can discover the pride of the Swiss industries, which are timepieces, which includes all major brands such as

Omega, Movado, Tag Heuer and many more, and this store also contains luxury jewelry and presents **Address: Rle des Anciens-Fossés 8, 1800 Vevey, Switzerland**

Culture and Festival in Interlaken

Interlaken, set in the heart of the Swiss Alps, provides a rich cultural tapestry woven from its history, customs, and dynamic community spirit. While Interlaken may be most known for its spectacular natural beauty and outdoor experiences, the town also celebrates a range of cultural events and festivals throughout the year. Here are some highlights of culture and events in Interlaken:

- **Swiss National Day (August 1st):**Celebrated in Switzerland, Swiss National Day celebrates the establishment of the Swiss

Confederation in 1291. In Interlaken, you may join in the festivities with traditional Swiss music, dance performances, fireworks, and cultural displays.

- **Trachtengruppe Interlaken:** The Trachtengruppe Interlaken is a local cultural organization committed to conserving and promoting traditional Swiss folk culture. Throughout the year, they offer events, concerts, and courses exhibiting Swiss music, dance, costumes, and traditions.

- **International Trucker & Country Festival**:Held annually in June, the International Trucker & Country Festival in Interlaken draws music aficionados from throughout the globe. This multi-day festival combines live performances by worldwide country music acts, line dancing, truck shows, and food vendors dishing up hearty Swiss and American cuisine.

- **Christmas Markets:**During the holiday season, Interlaken comes alive with lively Christmas markets providing handcrafted products, traditional Swiss foods, mulled wine, and seasonal entertainment. Visitors may peruse booths covered with dazzling lights and seasonal decorations, great for finding unique presents and soaking up the Christmas spirit.

- **Interlaken Music Festival**: Throughout the summer months, Interlaken holds a variety of music festivals exhibiting a varied range of musical genres, including classical, jazz, folk, and current. Whether you're a music lover or just seeking to enjoy some live entertainment, the Interlaken Music Festival provides something for everyone.

- **Alpine Cheese Festival**: Switzerland is famed for its cheese, and Interlaken commemorates this culinary history with the Alpine Cheese Festival. Held yearly throughout the summer months, this festival features a range of Swiss cheeses, including Emmental, Gruyère, and Raclette, along with cheese-making demonstrations, tastings, and cultural performances.

- **Local Markets and Fairs**:Throughout the year, Interlaken holds a variety of local markets and fairs where visitors may taste regional foods, peruse handcrafted items, and immerse themselves in the local culture. From farmers' markets selling fresh fruit to artisan markets showing handcrafted items, these events look into everyday life in Interlaken.

These cultural events and festivals provide visitors a unique chance to explore the rich past and traditions of Interlaken, while also celebrating the town's dynamic community spirit. Whether you're exploring the busy alleys of the Christmas markets or dancing the night away at a country music festival, Interlaken's cultural scene is guaranteed to make a lasting impression.

Nightlife in Interlaken

Nightlife in Interlaken is one of the most fascinating venues in Switzerland. And although it's traditionally a spot for outdoor experiences, Interlaken also boasts a very amazing nightlife scene! Nestled amid the Swiss Alps, you'll discover many locations to let free, or just enjoy a peaceful night out. So, where should you go after the sun goes down? Read on to learn our ideas about Nightlife in Interlaken!

Great Pubs, Bars, and Nightclubs to Meet the Locals There's no better way to get to know a new location than by meeting the people! And where can you meet them? At the neighborhood pubs and bars, of course! These establishments are a regular staple in the nighttime scene in Interlaken, so you're certain to encounter a few. They're also fantastic areas to rest after a day of touring or skiing.

Balmers Biergarten Grill & Chill

If you're a visitor to Balmer's Hostel, then you'll surely visit this place a few times! Balmer's Biergarten Grill & Chill is a fantastic location to either have a drink or get something to eat. It's an informal and cozy environment where you may meet individuals from all around the globe.

If you're here in the summer, it's a great location to drink in the fresh outdoors! But it's also not horrible if you have a chance to arrive in winter. In the winter months, it's turned into the Balmer's Wintergarten. Try their amazing fondue and Alpermacaronis! But if you simply want a drink, every hot beverage on the menu is worth a try.

Address: Hauptstrasse 23, 3800 Matten bei Interlaken, Switzerland

Phone: +41 33 822 19 61

Hüsi Bierhaus

Next up on our Nightlife in Interlaken itinerary is the Hüsi Bierhaus! And although they do offer a broad choice of craft brews, you can order other beverages as well. The cuisine is fairly excellent quality also so don't miss out on having a bite! But what about the nightlife in the Interlaken part? Well, they hold quite a few live concerts, international sports parties, and other events. There's always something going on!

Address: Postgasse 3, 3800 Interlaken, Switzerland

Phone: +41 33 823 23 32

The Barracuda Cafe & Bar

If you've ever wondered what it feels like to walk into a bar filled with a lot of new acquaintances, then go to The Barracuda Cafe & Bar! The workers here are famous and always make you feel welcome. They're renowned locally for their insane drinks, fantastic cuisine, and wild parties! But if you simply want to swing by for an afternoon coffee, they also come highly recommended.

Address: Hauptstrasse 16, 3800 Matten bei Interlaken, Switzerland

Brasserie17

Famous for their ribs and wings, Brasserie17 is certainly a site you shouldn't miss in Interlaken. With a large choice of tasty beers on tap, plus scrumptious cuisine, you'll undoubtedly find something to delight you. Brassiere17 is also a terrific venue for live music on the nights, and they're also quite consistent with their sports broadcasts! And if you're coming in summer, be sure to secure a position on the wonderful covered garden terrace!

Address: Rosenstrasse 17, 3800 Interlaken, Switzerland

Chapter 8

Practical Information

Here's some practical advice on currency and money concerns, safety precautions, and emergency contacts for visitors visiting Interlaken:

Currency and Money Matters:

- Currency: The official currency of Switzerland is the Swiss Franc (CHF). Euros are often not accepted for transactions, thus it's advised to convert your cash into Swiss Francs upon arrival.
- Exchange Rates: Currency exchange services are accessible in banks, exchange offices, and airports in Interlaken. Be aware that exchange

rates may fluctuate, so it's a good idea to compare prices before converting money.

- ATMs: ATMs are extensively accessible in Interlaken, notably in the town center and around important tourist sites. Most ATMs accept major credit and debit cards but be careful to check with your bank on any overseas transaction costs.

- Credit Cards: Credit cards like Visa, Mastercard, and American Express are frequently accepted in Interlaken, notably in hotels, restaurants, and bigger stores. However, smaller places may only take cash, so it's good to have some Swiss Francs for modest transactions.

- Tipping: Tipping is not mandatory in Switzerland, since a service fee is typically included in the bill. However, if you get great service, it's traditional to offer a little tip of roughly 5-10% of the overall price.

Safety Tips:

- General Safety: Interlaken is a generally secure place for vacationers, with low crime rates. However, it's always essential to take care and be cautious, particularly in popular tourist locations and at night.

- Outdoor Safety:If you intend to indulge in outdoor sports such as hiking, skiing, or paragliding, be sure to observe safety requirements, stick to established paths, and check weather conditions before starting.

- Water Safety: While Switzerland has magnificent lakes and rivers, always use care while swimming or engaging in water activities. Be mindful of water currents, underwater dangers, and designated swimming zones.

- Mountain Safety:If you intend to explore the mountains surrounding Interlaken, particularly the Jungfrau area, consider hiring a trained mountain guide for safety and navigation in alpine terrain.

- Health and Wellbeing:Switzerland offers a good quality of healthcare, but it's still wise to travel with travel insurance that includes medical coverage. Be careful you bring any required prescriptions and know the location of neighboring pharmacies and medical institutions.

Emergency Contacts:

- Emergency Services: In case of emergency, contact 112 for police, fire, or medical help. This number is toll-free and may be called from any phone, including mobile phones and landlines.

- Police: For non-emergency police help or to report a crime, you may call the local police station in Interlaken at +41 (0)33 827 35 11.
- Medical Assistance: For medical emergencies, including ambulance services, contact 144. The closest hospital to Interlaken is the Spital Interlaken, situated at Bernastrasse 28, 3800 Interlaken.
- Embassy Contacts:If you need help from your embassy or consulate while in Switzerland, contact the closest diplomatic office. For example, the U.S. Embassy in Bern may be contacted at +41 (0)31 357 70 11.

By keeping these practical ideas in mind, you may have a safe and hassle-free vacation to Interlaken,

Switzerland, and make the most of your travel experience.

7 Days Itinerary

Here's a proposed 7-day plan for experiencing Interlaken and its neighboring attractions:

Day 1: Arrival and Orientation

- Arrive at Interlaken and settle into your hotel.
- Take a leisurely walk around the town center, appreciating the lovely Swiss architecture and scenic surroundings.
- Visit the Höhematte Park for panoramic views of the surrounding mountains.
- Enjoy supper at a local restaurant and experience traditional Swiss food.

Day 2: Adventure in the Jungfrau Region

- Take an early morning train to Kleine Scheidegg, situated at the foot of the Eiger, Mönch, and Jungfrau mountains.
- Ride the Jungfrau Railway to Jungfraujoch, the "Top of Europe," and tour the Ice Palace and observation platform. - Enjoy lunch at one of the restaurants with spectacular alpine views.
- Return to Interlaken in the evening and rest after a day of high-altitude activity.

Day 3: Lake Thun and Lake Brienz

- Spend the day touring the charming lakeside villages of Thun and Brienz.
- Take a picturesque boat tour on Lake Thun, appreciating the surrounding mountains and attractive towns.
- Visit the Thun Castle and see its historical displays.

- In the afternoon, take a short train journey to Brienz and wander along the lakefront promenade.
- Optional: Visit the Ballenberg Open-Air Museum to learn about Swiss rural life and architecture.

Day 4: Outdoor Adventure

- Start the day with an amazing paragliding trip over Interlaken and the surrounding mountains. - After landing, hire a bike and pedal along the lovely Aare River to the adjacent village of Unterseen. -
- In the afternoon, ascend the Harder Kulm Panorama Trail for stunning views of Interlaken and the Jungfrau region. -
- Enjoy a quiet evening at a nearby spa or wellness facility.

Day 5: Explore Lauterbrunnen Valley

- Take a day excursion to the gorgeous Lauterbrunnen Valley, noted for its breathtaking waterfalls and cliffs.
- Visit the Trümmelbach Falls, a sequence of cascading waterfalls within a mountain canyon.
- Explore the quaint hamlet of Wengen and take a spectacular cable car journey to the summit of the Mannlichen mountain for panoramic views of the surrounding peaks.
- Return to Interlaken in the evening and relax with supper at a nice restaurant.

Day 6: Grindelwald and First - Travel to the alpine hamlet of Grindelwald and take the cable car to the FiMountain.

- Enjoy exhilarating activities such as the First Flyer zip line, First Glider, and Cliff Walk.

- Hike the scenic Bachalpsee Lake route fo breathtaking views of the Eiger, Mönch, and Jungfrau mountains.
- Return to Interlaken in the evening and eat a goodbye supper at a classic Swiss restaurant.

Day 7: Departure - Enjoy a leisurely breakfast and enjoy one more walk around the streets of Interlaken.

- Depending on your departure schedule, explore any remaining attractions or gift stores.
- Check out of your hotel and leave from Interlaken, bringing with you memories of a wonderful Swiss vacation.

17. Can you suggest a decent restaurant? - Können Sie ein gutes Restaurant empfehlen?

18. What time is it? - Wie spät ist es?

19. Where is the rail station? - Wo ist der Bahnhof?

20. How do I go to [destination]? - Wie komme ich nach [Ziel]?

21. Can I get the bill, please? - Kann ich die Rechnung haben, bitte?

22. What's your name? - Wie ist Ihr Name?

23. My name is [Name]. - Mein Name ist [Name].

24. Where are you from? - Woher kommen Sie?

25. I'm from [country]. - Ich komme aus [Land].

26. Cheers! - Prost!

27. How's the weather today? - Wie ist das Wetter heute?

28. What's the Wi-Fi password? - Wie ist das WLAN-Passwort?

29. Can I have a glass of water, please? - Kann ich bitte ein Glas Wasser haben?

30. Have a wonderful day! - Einen schönen Tag noch!

Conclusion

Embark on a trip to Interlaken, where every moment is an adventure and every perspective a masterpiece. From the towering peaks of the Swiss Alps to the calm beaches of its crystal-clear lakes, Interlaken calls with its compelling allure and unlimited possibilities. Whether you're seeking adrenaline-pumping thrills, calm moments of introspection, or cultural immersion in the heart of Switzerland, Interlaken provides an amazing experience that will leave you wishing to return. So pack your luggage, take in the fresh mountain air, and let Interlaken fire your spirit of wonder and discovery. Your Swiss adventure awaits!"

Printed in Dunstable, United Kingdom